TESTIMONIALS

"Clarity about contracts and laws is a fundamental part of consumer protection. A book that helps Maryland consumers understand their rights and obligations in HOA and condo communities—without needing a law degree—is an important contribution to the field."

- Marceline White, Executive Director, Maryland Consumer Rights Coalition

"As the primary sponsor of the 2005 Senate bill that created the 2005–2006 Maryland Task Force on Common Ownership Communities, I welcome this consumer guide, which provides greatly needed nontechnical education to both boards of condos and HOAs, as well as to rank-and-file homeowners in these communities."

- Senator Delores G. Kelley

"In a day of confusing, ever-changing, and hard-to-follow Maryland condo and HOA law, homeowners and association board members need a clear reference guide to all the important things they need to know."

- Boyd McGinn, Realtor, associate broker, RE/MAX 100

"As a member of the Maryland General Assembly serving on the committee that addresses real estate issues, I know full well how great a need there is for this publication, which addresses HOA and condo laws in plain and clear language.

"As a resident for 26 years in an HOA in Columbia, I also know what a positive impact a clear understanding of these laws can have on the lives of HOA and condo residents."

- Delegate Elizabeth Bobo, Maryland House of Delegates

"Some of the most confusing law on the books references HOAs and condo associations. A reference guide to untangle the legal terminology is a blessing for most home and condo owners. As a member of the Housing and Real Property Subcommittee, I have been in the forefront of proposed new legislation and have found Jeanne Ketley a valuable resource for HOA and condo issues."

- Pamela G. Beidle, Maryland House of Delegates

Happy Homes:

*A Consumer's Guide to Maryland Condo and HOA Law
and Best Practices for Homeowners and Boards*

Senator Kelley :
    In appreciation for
your service to Maryland
Consumers.

Jeanne Ketley
6/13/14

By

Jeanne N. Ketley Ph.D.

ISBN: 1497520622

ISBN 13: 9781497520622

Contents

Contents

Acknowledgments

Many people have helped make this consumer guide a reality. Foremost is my partner, Jan Bowman, a talented short story writer. I thank Jan for reviewing the initial "Condo Corners" as well as portions of this book and making the text clearer and more readable.

I also thank Patti Laidig, Columbia Town Center's village manager, for having the foresight to realize that articles clarifying Maryland condo/HOA law would be of benefit to Town Center condominium residents and agreeing to publish my short articles in the Town Center monthly newsletter, *The Centerfold*. Once the articles were finished, I realized that I had the beginnings of a book that could really be helpful to anyone living in a condominium association or homeowners association.

My fellow MHA Executive Committee members have also been important to the clarity of *Happy Homes*. Insights gained from MHA Executive Committee member discussions of Maryland condo/HOA problems helped shape this book. I especially thank MHA First Vice-President Rand Fishbein and MHA Second Vice-President Kamala Edwards for their important insights. I also thank Executive Committee members Clara Perlingiero, Cindy Trost, Pat Wigginton, David Bosworth, Sharlene Deskins, Walter Gold, and Abbott Roseman for their contributions to MHA discussions. Discussions with past Executive Committee members Arlene

Perkins, James Blasic, and Jack Wallace added clarity to this book.

I thank Peter Drymalski for his help with the history of MHA and Rebecca G. Bowman for her review of the final manuscript.

Additionally, I thank Professor Evan McKenzie, whose books *Privatopia* and *Beyond Privatopia* helped me realize the need in Maryland for a book such as *Happy Homes*.

Finally, I thank my editor and publishing consultant, Allyson Machate, and web developer and online marketing consultant Angela Render for invaluable help in making this book a reality.

To the Memory of Dot Sager

Common ownership communities (COCs) are legal entities organized as nonprofit small businesses. Before the enactment of laws that specifically govern them, Maryland COCs were incorporated and were governed by the Corporations and Associations Article in the Maryland Code (specifically, Titles 2, 4, 4A, and 5). Corporate law was created to protect the personal assets of the individuals who form corporations  and to protect assets of the corporation such as trade secrets from others. Corporations, including incorporated COCs, were therefore allowed to make decisions and take action in closed meetings out of the view of the public.

Dorothy (Dot) Sager, a retired Montgomery County math teacher living in a condominium in Rockville, Maryland, thought it was outrageous that corporate law governed her condominium and that her board could take actions in secret. She decided to change that. In 1981, she organized an advocacy group called the Montgomery County Condominium Association (MCCA). The organization ultimately operated statewide and the name was then changed to Maryland Homeowners' Association (MHA).

In 1983, MHA, under Dot Sager's leadership, urged the governor and the Maryland legislature to reinstate the Maryland State Commission on Condominiums, Cooperatives and Homeowners to provide better protections for homeowners in state law. When the commission was reactivated, the governor invited Dot Sager to be a member. This commission was responsible for creating the current Maryland Condominium Act (MCA) and the Maryland Homeowners Association Act (MHAA). These acts were modified in 1998 to add additional homeowner rights. Over the years to the present date, MHA has supported additional homeowner protections guaranteed by state law.

In 1987, MHA and Dot Sager also lobbied for the formation of the Montgomery County Commission on Common Ownership Communities (CCOC) to provide education for those living in association environments and provide mediation in shared ownership communities in Montgomery County. This commission still exists, and other Maryland counties are considering similar commissions using the CCOC as a model.

I had the privilege of meeting Dot Sager. In her last year, the MHA Executive Committee held its meetings at Leisure World, where Dot was living, so Dot could attend MHA meetings. Although she was in a wheelchair at the time, you could see fire in her eyes when the group discussed stories of homeowner injustices in condos and homeowners associations (HOAs).

Usually there were lots of people chatting with Dot before the MHA meeting began. On this evening, both Dot and I arrived at the meeting room quite early and we were the only people there. Dot looked at me and said, "You're working very hard."

To the Memory of Dot Sager

Without thinking, I answered, "That's because I want to be the next Dot Sager."

She looked at me for a while and said, "You know, I was your age when I started."

Dot Sager died on February 12, 2005, at age 89.

Introduction

I've lived in several condominium associations and for a long time happily left the running of things to the elected board of directors. I had a demanding job and a young son to raise, and I felt lucky not to have to deal with the annoyance of arranging exterior maintenance and property insurance because someone else would handle that and more.

Then one day a tree fell on the roof of my condominium townhome and slid down the back of my house, smashing the roof gutter, marking the back of the house, and smashing a privacy fence and the deck of my town house and everything on the deck. I tried to submit a claim under our community's master insurance for the portion of the damage that was covered by the master insurance. It was quite a shock when the property manager and board told me they would not submit the claim and that in fact I had to pay to repair the damage.

Slowly the ugly side of condominium living became more apparent.

It began with conversations. I spoke with several other condo owners in my community and in other communities. According to those more informed than I, it appeared that my board was illegally making decisions about who could and could not submit insurance claims. Worse, our management company had been following the board's directives rather than the letter of the law.

I did not immediately assume that anyone had ill intentions. Rather, it all seemed to be a misunderstanding. So I wrote letters to both the board and the manager explaining their error. Much to my amazement, the Board went to the extreme of spending $1,000 of association money for an attorney to write a response aimed at convincing me that the damage to my property was my problem and not the association's responsibility, despite the explanations and legal references I'd shared with them. Unfortunately, they did not send this letter to me—only to the management company, which simply told me they would not file a claim because they had "an attorney letter" justifying a lack of response. It took several certified letters to the management company requesting a copy of this letter until I finally received it.

Fortunately, a neighbor of mine had insurance experience and when I described the battle I had unwittingly entered into, she recommended that I file a complaint with the Maryland Insurance Administration. Within days of filing the complaint, I received a notice from my association's management company informing me that the association master policy would, after all, pay for repairs.

So here it was: The board had misled me, an association manager had misled me, and even their attorney had tried to further their position—out of ignorance or willfully in spite of the law I'll never know. If not for the Maryland Insurance Administration, I would have had to hire my own attorney and pay thousands of dollars just to get a valid claim paid.

Many years passed, but I never forgot that experience. After retiring from my career with the National Institutes of Health, I started looking for a way to contribute to the betterment of my community. I came across the website of the Maryland Homeowners' Association (MHA). Here was a statewide group dedicated to protecting the rights of homeowners living in condominium associations and home-owners associations. I wondered how many other people like me had fallen victim to uninformed boards and management companies. I began attending MHA meetings and found that my experience was, sadly, rather common. It quickly became clear to me that most Maryland boards and homeowners have no idea what their rights and responsibilities are or how the Maryland Condominium and Homeowners Association Acts affect them.

I joined MHA and eventually served as an MHA vice president and, later, president. In that capacity, I spent ten years advising homeowners and boards by responding to telephone or e-mailed inquiries about ways to deal with their condo/HOA problems. This gave me another perspective. Testifying in favor of condominium unit owner and homeowner rights bills in Annapolis forced me to learn how to understand legislative language. I'm a scientist with a PhD in physiological chemistry, so I'm used to understanding complicated concepts and working with language that to others may seem unclear. Even so, my legislative understanding took a while. It seems to me that "legalese" is written so that only attorneys understand it (and, as my own experiences attest, sometimes not even they know what they're reading!).

Given the vast gap between the existing laws and the ability of most people to access and/or fully understand the restrictions and protections governing their communities, I eventually embarked on a new project, which you now hold in your hands. My goal is simple: I want to help you, the unit owner or homeowner, to live in peaceful, happy coexistence with your neighbors and your community associations. This book is my translation of Maryland condominium and HOA law into what I hope is easily understandable prose. Translating these comprehensive laws entirely would result in a practically unreadable tome that would overwhelm the average reader. Instead, I've focused on the most common points of contention and the issues that, in my experience, would contribute substantially to the happiness of all involved if better understood. To that end, I offer some best practices as well.

Please note that this book is not a substitute for competent legal advice. However, it gives you a fighting chance at understanding what your association boards, managers, and attorneys are talking about and enough guidance on where and how to challenge them, if necessary. Throughout I reference specific portions of the law so you can research further at your convenience. I also point you in the direction of resources that can help you if you find yourself in conflict with your association's representatives.

During my time with the MHA, I once heard a story about a manager who insisted that it was okay to hold private board meetings via e-mail as long as any decisions made were announced later at an open meeting. When challenged, the manager replied, "Lots of lawyers said it was okay." Since you were smart enough to buy this book, if anyone tried to mislead you in this way, you would simply show that person the section titled "Openness and Transparency" in Chapter 2. You could even point out the direct references to where in the MCA and/or the MHAA it says that all board meetings must be open and announced. If that fails, you could turn to the Resources section at the end of this book and contact any of the listed organizations for assistance.

Let us all remember that board members are our neighbors—there is no "us" and "them" when it comes to dealing with community associations. Therefore, this book aims to educate existing and future board members as well. It is especially important that boards of directors adhere to local, state, and federal law, for both the sake of their community and their own protection. Directors have the responsibility to protect millions of dollars' worth of real estate—they must have the highest ethical standards. Moreover, liability insurance does not usually protect directors if they violate the law, whether knowingly or out of ignorance.

Since state laws do change, I will update this book yearly. The book in your hands is as of 2013. I will also post regular updates at www.jeanneketley.com, so check in often to stay on top of current policies and legislative efforts. The MHA website, www.marylandhomeownersassociation.info, is another place to check.

Reading this book is a first step, not the last. You must find time to help manage your association. Run for the board or ask to be appointed to committees. I know of a condominium association that had only two board members when the community's bylaws called for seven. All the decisions that board made could have been challenged because of the lack of a quorum. This community finally woke up and now has a full board.

Rather than sitting and grumbling, use your power to make your community what you want it to be. Ultimately, the success of your association in creating "Happy Homes" depends on you.

Jeanne N. Ketley, PhD

Columbia, Maryland

Definitions

The Maryland Condominium Act (MCA; also called "the Condo Act") and the Maryland Homeowners Association Act (MHAA; also called "the HOA Act") each begin with a definition of terms. The Maryland Condominium Act is codified in the Maryland Real Property Code, Sections 11B 101 et seq. For simplification, however, I will refer to specific sections of those acts as MCA 11-xxx or MHAA 11B-xxx throughout this book. Some of the meanings are obvious and some are not. I've also included some definitions of my own. Here is a list of the meanings of the less obvious terms:

Unit owner: If you own an apartment, town house, and so on, in a condominium, you are a "unit owner" in the condominium association. If there are 100 units in the condominium association and you own one unit, then you own 1/100 of the association's *common elements* (defined shortly) and are responsible for 1/100 of the association's common expenses. The living space in your unit belongs exclusively to you. The association owns your walls and roof. See the following definition of *lot owner* and notice how condominium ownership is very different from HOA ownership.

Council of unit owners: All the unit owners form the *council*, which is the governing body for the condominium. Since it is hard to govern if the entire council must meet and vote on issues, this responsibility is usually delegated to an elected board of directors. In an HOA, the homeowners association, board of directors, or other entity established to govern the development is simply called a *governing body* (defined shortly).

Lot owner: If you live in an HOA, you own a *lot* (the land your home is standing on) and Maryland law refers to you as a *lot owner*. Many times the term *member of the homeowner association* is used instead of *lot owner*. As a member of an HOA, you own a portion of all the common property but also own the structural elements of your home such as the walls and roof.

Governing body: The governing body is the council of unit or lot owners *or* the board of directors, depending on what's stated in the governing documents. Since it is difficult to govern with every unit or lot owner having a voice in every decision, the governing documents usually give governance authority, within specified limits, to the elected board of directors.

Governing document: Governing documents are the documents required by the MCA and the MHAA that specify how the association is organized and governed. These documents include the public offering statement, the declaration, the plat, the bylaws, and the rules and regulations.

Board of directors: The board of directors is composed of the owners that the association members elect to govern the association. It is sometimes called "the board" or "the BOD" for short.

General common elements: The general common elements are all of the property that is not owned by individual unit owners but rather owned by all the members together. In a condominium, this is usually the parking lot, your sidewalks, paved paths, and open land. If you are in a multilevel condominium building, it might include things like the elevators, hallways, and a common meeting space. The association's governing documents must state what parts of the property are common elements. In an HOA community, it is all the property outside your home and lot that is owned and maintained by the HOA, such as green space or a communal swimming pool.

Limited common elements: In a condominium, limited common elements are those identified in the declaration or on the condominium plat as reserved for the exclusive use of one or more but less than all of the unit owners. An example would be a balcony on a condominium that is reserved for the exclusive use of the condominium owner. Governing documents vary as to whether limited common elements are maintained by the unit owner or by the condominium association. There is no comparable category in the MHAA.

Common expenses and common profits: The money taken in (common profits) and the bills that must be paid (common expenses) related to common property.

Electronic transmission: Any form of communication that does not involve the physical transmission of paper, that creates a record that:

- may be retained, retrieved, and reviewed by a recipient of the communication

- may be reproduced directly in paper form by a recipient through an automated process (for example, e-mail)

Occupant: You and your family or anyone who lives in your home as a renter or as a guest.

Percentage interests: (condominiums only) The percentage of the whole condominium that you are responsible for maintaining. For example, if utilities are a common expense, sometimes governing documents will state that because a two-bedroom condo generally uses more utilities than a one-bedroom condo, the two-bedroom unit will pay a larger monthly assessment.

Unit: Your condominium home, technically a three-dimensional space identified as such in the declaration and on the condominium plat. A unit may include two or more noncontiguous spaces. If you live in a multilevel condominium, an example of a noncontiguous space would be your home and a storage space in the basement.

Management company or manager: While not defined in the MCA or the MHAA, associations often employ a person or company to handle the day-to-day operation of the property. The manager is selected, hired, and supervised by the BOD and ensures that unit owners or homeowners comply with association rules and regulations. Best practices for hiring management companies are included in Appendix 1.

CHAPTER 1

Rights and Responsibilities

How many people living in Columbia's Town Center know that they live in three common ownership communities (COCs), each with its own set of covenants? Not very many, in my experience. For most residents, the most important association for their personal financial health and happiness is the one they send their monthly condo fees to—their own condo association. But the Town Center Association and the greater Columbia Association also govern them.

The general concept of sharing common property can be traced back to eighteenth-century England, when the Earl of Leicester wanted to preserve a fenced-in park in Leicester Square in London and asked the owners of the residential lots surrounding the park to pay a tax for its upkeep. In 1808, the next owner sold the park with a restrictive covenant saying that the new owner and his "heirs and assigns" must keep the park as is.[1] This may have been one of the first restrictive covenants ever recorded.

The covenant concept was then transported to the United States in 1831 when Samuel Ruggles drained a swamp in Manhattan and laid it out like London Square, complete with a gate and an iron fence around it. Only the owners of homes around the square had keys to the gate. He called it Gramercy Park and the title to the park went to trustees who were told to maintain it for the benefit of those who owned the surrounding homes.[2]

Another piece of planned community history is our own Greenbelt, Maryland. In the late 1930s, Greenbelt was one of three "green belt" town projects initiated by President Franklin D. Roosevelt's Resettlement Administration. These towns were to be a model for future town planning in America that would combine the best aspects of rural life (lakes, woods, and open spaces) with aspects of urban life (recreational facilities, theaters, and shops). Construction for Greenbelt started in the fall of 1935.[3] Modern Greenbelt is now a city with an elected mayor and a city council.

Planned communities grew and grew, and today 1,045,000 Marylanders live in common ownership communities in Maryland.

---

1 Evan McKenzie, *Privatopia: Homeowner Associations and the Rise of Residential Private Government* (New Haven, CT: Yale University Press), 34.
2 *Ibid.*
3 Greenbelt Museum, *www.greenbeltmuseum.org.*

Maryland Association Data*

- 5,226 Maryland common ownership communities (COCs)
- 1,045,000 Marylanders live in COCs
- 34,000 Marylanders serve on a COC board of directors
- $69 billion is the value of homes in Maryland COCs
- $696 million is the annual operating revenue for Maryland COCs
- $609 million is held in investment accounts for long-term maintenance of Maryland COCs

*Estimates are based on U.S. Census and Community Associations Institute statistics, published in the CAI Maryland Legislative Action Committee brochure (rev. 01/11).

Rights and Responsibilities of Homeowners

With the growth of COCs came problems that led to the need for and enactment of the Maryland Condominium Act and the Maryland Homeowners Association Act. There is also a body of other federal, state, and local law that guides HOA and condominium governance. Dealing with all these separate sets of rules and ruling bodies can be a headache, but you can lessen your pain and aggravation if you begin with a solid understanding of your basic rights and responsibilities.

Unit owners and homeowners have the right to:

1. Receive fair and respectful treatment by the board of directors, managers, and contractors.
2. Participate in governing their community association by attending meetings, running for election to the board, and serving on committees.
3. See how their association money is spent.

4. Live in a community where the property is maintained according to the bylaws and the rules and regulations.
5. Receive fair treatment regarding association obligations.
6. Receive and review all documents related to the community association as allowed by law.
7. Appeal to the board of directors any decision that affects them adversely.

As always, the privileges and rights we enjoy under the law are accompanied by certain obligations. All unit owners and homeowners have the responsibility to:

1. Pay assessments on time.
2. Maintain their property as described in the rules and regulations.
3. Treat the board of directors, the association manager, contractors, and all neighbors with respect.
4. Be familiar with the association's governing documents and rules and regulations.
5. Obey the governing rules and regulations.
6. Ensure that renters, relatives, and friends adhere to community rules and regulations.
7. Vote in all elections in person or by proxy.
8. Serve on committees and run for the board of directors.
9. Work at making the community a good place to live.

Rights and Responsibilities of Board Members

The popular press constantly highlights stories of boards of directors abusing their power. For example, a story in the November 21, 2013, WLEX news in Lexington, Kentucky, reported that a woman lost her completely paid-for home after her HOA foreclosed to collect $300 in fees. She says she never received any warning letters. While liens are a useful threat for boards that have difficulty collecting fair assessments and other fees from community members, it's pretty frightening that something like this can happen in this country. A board always has other means to force the collection of unpaid debts. Foreclosure should always be last on the list.

But that doesn't mean a board should never take action. As a representative entity, every board of directors has its own set of rights and responsibilities to follow. Board members have the right to expect:

1. Owners to pay their assessments on time.
2. Residents, resident guests, and renters to comply with the community's rules and regulations.
3. Respectful interactions with residents, resident guests, and renters.
4. Privacy at home.
5. That they are appreciated as a policy-making body leaving the day-to-day work of the association to hired staff and contractors.
6. Respectful interactions with managers and contractors.

Like the duties of homeowners, the duties of the condo or HOA board are described in the governing documents. Beyond those legal obligations, I recommend several other board practices such as "seek to keep the community informed" and "solicit owner feedback before important decisions are made" that seem to me to be just common sense. Thus, Board members have the responsibility to:

1. Collect and spend association money wisely.
2. Monitor all association accounts.
3. Conduct fair elections.

4. Conduct all business in a transparent manner, as required by law.
5. Make sure attendees at open meetings feel welcome.
6. Listen respectfully to owners on issues related to the association.
7. Treat managers and contractors with respect.
8. Solicit owner feedback before important decisions are made.
9. Avoid conflicts of interest.
10. Avoid the appearance of a conflict of interest.
11. Seek to keep the community informed.
12. Use foreclosure to collect fees only as a very last resort.

In summary, the key to a content community seems to boil down to the Golden Rule: Do unto others as you would have them do unto you. This applies to both board members and homeowners. Sounds simple but it's not, which is why new state laws regulating common ownership communities get passed every year.

CHAPTER 2

Who Has Access to What?

The aim of this chapter is to describe practices that foster openness and transparency. Not only are these practices reflected in condo governing documents but also many of these practices are part of federal, state, and local law. But really, openness and transparency benefits everyone and prevents a lot of unnecessary strife. Sometimes failure to keep the community informed just gives grist to the community rumor mill, but I think we all know how much trouble that can be when it's all cranked up.

For example, in one of my neighboring communities, land-scaping replacements were made close to a board member's home. Many in the community assumed this was an example of that board member misusing his authority to his advantage. The truth was that these necessary repairs were a part of a larger community project. Had a "landscaping replacements pending" notice gone out to the community by e-mail or other means, this misunderstanding could have been avoided, and a lot of ill will besides.

Openness and Transparency

One example of how the law promotes openness and transparency can be found in MCA 11-109(c)(6) and MHAA 11B-111(1). This section states that all board meetings must be open, and the time and place must be announced in advance to all owners. That means a board may not make decisions via teleconference or e-mail voting, or during unannounced meetings. The exception would be a teleconference where the conference phone is at a location that is open and announced such that any homeowner could listen to the discussion.

The intent of this law is to ensure that all condo and lot owners are protected in their right to be present during any discussion involving the security of their home. If the home-owner has an opinion on the subject being considered, they can voice that opinion during the board meeting's open session.

There are situations, however, when a board meeting may be closed. Both MCA 11-109.1 and MHAA 11B-111(4) list the reasons a board meeting may be closed. The only difference between the two acts is that in the MHAA, the reasons for closing a meeting also apply to a committee of the home-owners association. Board meetings may be closed only for the following:

1. Discussion of matters pertaining to employees and personnel;
2. Protection of the privacy or reputation of individuals in matters not related to the governing body's business;
3. Consultation with legal counsel on legal matters;

4. Consultation with staff personnel, consultants, attorneys, board members, or other persons in connection with pending or potential litigation or other legal matters;
5. Investigative proceedings concerning possible or actual criminal misconduct;
6. Consideration of the terms or conditions of a business transaction in the negotiation stage if the disclosure could adversely affect the economic interests of the governing body;
7. Complying with a specific constitutional, statutory, or judicially imposed requirement protecting particular proceedings or matters from public disclosure; or
8. Discussion of individual owner assessment accounts.

A statement of the time, place, and purpose of any closed meeting, the record of the vote of each board member by which any meeting was closed, and the reason for closing the meeting must be included in the minutes of the next meeting of the board.

Unless one of these issues needs to be discussed, you have the right to attend board meetings and have any decisions made at board meetings reflected in the minutes. If you can't be at the board meeting, you should examine the minutes of all board meetings to see what actions have been taken. All major decisions must be in board meeting minutes in order for the action to be legally valid. Even if a board decision is made in an emergency situation, that decision must be recorded in the minutes of the next board meeting. For most busy people, examining board minutes are the only way to keep informed of what's happening in their association.

Access to Financial Statements and Meeting Minutes

Ever wonder how your assessment fees are spent? A recent change to Maryland law gives you the right to review the same financial statements that your community's management company prepares regularly for your board. You can request copies of these and any other recent financial reports by contacting your board or management company and requesting this information in writing.

MCA 11-116 and MHAA 11B-112 state that the requested information must be sent to you by mail, electronic transmission, or personal delivery within twenty-one days after receipt of the written request. The maximum charge that can be made for providing these financial statements in print form must not "exceed the limits authorized under Title 7, Subtitle 2 of the Courts Article," which is currently $0.50 per page. The names of owners in arrears will be withheld out of respect for privacy concerns.

Unfortunately, unless you are an accountant, these statements are sometimes difficult to understand, but with a little practice, you can figure them out. The financial report, sometimes called *the financials*, is provided to your board of directors by the manager monthly.

The financial report usually covers one month and gives the balances in the association's accounts as of the end of the month. Many reports also provide a cumulative report of what was spent during the year. For a general idea of the financial health of your community, look at the balances that are in the checking account and all reserve accounts. Reserve accounts consist of the money being saved for future major repairs. If you want to know what was spent for the month, go to the checking register page. It will tell you how much was spent that month for items such as insurance, landscaping, legal fees, and the management fee, among others.

There is no reason why any HOA or condo owner should say, "I don't know where my assessment money is going." All you need to do is receive your association's monthly financial report to keep abreast of the financial stability of your association.

Maryland law also requires boards to provide approved meeting minutes within twenty-one days of a written request. However, most minutes only record the specific actions voted on at a board meeting. If you want to know everything that is discussed and who said what, you'll need to attend the meeting. The minimum number of times a board must meet each year is in your governing documents. To keep the business of the association moving, most boards meet once a month. Since each meeting's minutes are officially approved at the following meeting, many boards release a draft copy of the minutes in the interim. Keep in mind that this draft is unedited and may change because of board member corrections.

To monitor what's going on in your association, always request copies of your board meeting minutes. These can be sent to you as an e-mail attachment and thus cost the association almost nothing. Any board that refuses you access to meeting minutes has something to hide. If this happens to you, file a complaint with the appropriate federal, state, or county agency. See Chapter 4 and the Resources section at the end of this book for more information on filing complaints.

Right of Access to Books and Records

Did you know that MCA 11-116 and MHAA 11B-112 protect every homeowner's right to have access to all the books and records of his or her association? The acts state that with only a few exceptions, all records, including insurance policies and signed contracts, must be made available by the association for examination or copying, or both, by any owner during normal business hours and after reasonable notice.

Typically, your association manager will keep these records. If you wish to see them, Maryland law states that you must send your request in writing. If it is too costly for the manager to copy and send the requested information, it may be cheaper for you to arrange to go to the management office and do your own copying. These materials must be made available within fifteen days of a written request. The manager or association may impose a reasonable fee for the labor involved in assembling this information, but having an attorney assemble the materials is neither a reasonable expense nor necessary. Ask in advance what the charges are. If you are told that an attorney must sit with you while you are reviewing records, file a complaint with a governmental agency against your association. See Chapter 4 and the Resources section at the end of this book for where and how to file a complaint.

There are just a few exceptions to what information or materials you may access under the acts because of privacy concerns. Both MCA 11-116(c)(3) and MHAA 11B-112 give the following reasons why records may be withheld:

Books and records kept by or on behalf of a council of unit owners (or homeowners association) may be withheld from public inspection, except for inspection by the person who is the subject of the record or the person's designee or guardian, to the extent that they concern:

1. Personnel records, not including information on individual salaries, wages, bonuses, and other compensation paid to employees;
2. An individual's medical records;

3. An individual's personal financial records, including assets, income, liabilities, net worth, bank balances, financial history or activities, and creditworthiness;
4. Records relating to business transactions that are currently in negotiation;
5. The written advice of legal counsel; or
6. Minutes of a closed meeting of the board of directors or other governing body of the council of unit owners, unless a majority of a quorum of the board of directors or governing body that held the meeting approves unsealing the minutes or a recording of the minutes for public inspection.

Except for a reasonable charge imposed on a person desiring to review or copy the books and records or who requests delivery of information, the council of unit owners (or homeowners association) may not impose any charges under this section.

CHAPTER 3

How Rules Are Made and Changed

Do you ever look around your neighborhood and see something that bothers you and wish there were an association rule forbidding such things?

Well-thought-out rules and regulations can add serenity to a community so that homeowners can have the peaceful enjoyment of their homes. Most communities update rules and regulations periodically. However, there are three very important points to keep in mind when formulating rules:

1. Be reasonable.
2. Do not propose any rule you can't enforce.
3. Involve the entire community early on in the rule-making process.

In my town house neighborhood, a couple of kids would always leave their bicycles anywhere they dropped them for the night. One of the spots was in a neighbor's parking spot.

This poor guy would get home late at night and even though he was exhausted, he would have to get out of his car to remove bicycles from his spot before being able to park his car. Talking to the kids' parents didn't help. A community rule that said children's bikes and toys must not be left unattended on paths and parking lots did the trick, though.

Did this cure the problem 100 percent of the time? No, because kids will be kids. But it definitely made the occurrences fewer and farther between, because with the new rule, parents could be sanctioned or fined for failing to appropriately deal with their children's actions. This encouraged more parents to talk to their kids about where they left their belongings and likewise encouraged more responsibility among the neighborhood children.

And here's where the "be reasonable" comes in. Don't expect 100 percent compliance 100 percent of the time. We're all human.

Order of Precedence of Laws and Documents

There is a common misperception that if a board just follows its own governing documents, everything will be fine. Not necessarily so. There are federal, state, and county laws that supersede association governing documents. If state law and condo or HOA governing documents conflict, which has precedence?

The law is clear on this issue. The order of precedence of the laws that govern one's home are as follows:

1. Federal law and federal court decisions.
2. State law and state court decisions. The state laws include:
   - The Condominium Act
   - The Homeowners Association Act

- The Maryland Contract Lien Act, Real Property Article, Sections 14-201 to 14-206

- The Corporations and Associations Article in the Maryland Code, Titles 1–12

3. Local law, regulations, and court decisions.
4. Your association's declaration and covenants, conditions, and restrictions (CCRs).
5. Your association's bylaws.
6. Your association's rules and regulations and board resolutions.

Because of this order of precedence, there is no need to redo governing documents every year because of new or amended local, state, or federal laws. However, it is wise to keep your community informed of all changes in the law and that they understand how the new law may negate something in the existing governing documents. For example, some older communities still have outdated governing documents banning people of certain racial groups or ethnicities from purchasing a home in the community. Such a stipulation would be overruled by more recent legislation.

So that community members understand what they can and cannot do, some associations have "translated" the important restrictive covenants in the governing documents into a few pages that are easy to understand and distribute this document to the community.

Condominium Rule-Making Procedure

Changing times may prompt you or your board to want to add new sections to your association's rules and regulations and/ or remove old sections. Sometimes proposed rule changes or additions arise more naturally from circumstances in the community or the experiences of our neighboring communities. The best way to initiate changes to the rules and regulations is for the board to appoint a committee of unit owners to draft the new rules. Once the committee is finished and the board has had its input, by law the board must send a draft of the proposed rule to the entire community for comments and an open meeting held to discuss the new rules.

MCA 11-111 outlines the procedure that must be followed in order for the rule to be finalized:

1. The board/manager must send a letter with the proposed rule and specified start date to all unit owners at least fifteen days before an open meeting is convened to discuss the proposed rule.

2. The letter must state that unit owners can submit written comments and/or speak at this open meeting. This is a wonderful opportunity for a board to show that it cares about the opinions of the unit owners. All unit owners must be allowed to speak, and it is up to the board chairperson to make sure no one person dominates. The board must be open to making changes in the text and then vote on the changed text. If the changes get too complex, the vote will need to wait until another draft is prepared.

3. After considering unit owner comments, and if no changes are suggested, the board will vote in open session to accept or reject the new rule or rule change.

If some unit owners object to the board's decision to implement the new rule, a procedure is available to *negate* the rule in question is as follows:

1. To initiate a vote to negate the new rule, 15 percent of the unit owners must sign and file a petition for a special meeting *within fifteen days* of the open meeting.
2. The rule is not valid unless this special meeting is held. This is to ensure that the board doesn't just ignore the petition.
3. A quorum (as defined in the association bylaws) of unit owners must attend this special meeting. Although not specified, presumably proxies can be used.
4. If at least 50 percent of the unit owners who are present at that meeting disapprove the rule, and if they represent 33 percent of the total votes of the condominium, the rule is considered void.
5. Any unit owner can ask for an exception to a rule, but the request must be done in writing to the board within thirty days of a rule's passage.

This process ensures that all condo owners have a voice in the creation of the rules that govern their community. Notice that if you want to challenge the new rule, the challenge process has strict timelines. As mentioned earlier, a petition for a special meeting to negate the new rule must be filed within fifteen days of its approval.

Maryland legislation has been proposed to have this procedure apply to HOAs as well as condo associations, and most savvy attorneys recommend that their HOA clients adopt the condominium procedure now. I encourage homeowners to contact their elected Maryland representatives and make it clear that you want the same protections as condo owners. Alternatively and in the meantime, HOAs can amend their bylaws to include a similar rule-making procedure.

Many of the complaints received by MHA revolve around whether five people (a board) have a right to give orders to everyone else. To avoid conflict in your HOA, always involve as many people as possible in rule making. To avoid conflict in your condominium association, follow Maryland's rule-making law.

Amending Bylaws

When first written, community association bylaws were put in place to create the association and a governance system. The bylaws, however, were also written to protect the developer. If your development is thirty years old and the "transition" to owner governance is complete, language protecting the developer is no longer needed. Further, older bylaws may have covenants that are now offensive and illegal, such as not allowing people of certain ethnicities to purchase a home in the community. Bylaws are a living document and occasionally need to be changed.

An action to amend association bylaws is costly because of the legal fees involved and should be done only when absolutely necessary. Since federal, state, and county law supersedes anything in association bylaws, there is no need to amend bylaws simply because of changed laws.

Also, never allow an attorney to completely rewrite your bylaws. There is the possibility that instead of reviewing your bylaws and seeing what would be suitable for your association, an attorney will use a bylaws draft from another association and have a clerk do a search and replace on the association name. Or, it is possible an attorney could put in language beneficial to the attorney rather than the community.

In 2012 MHA received a copy of a proposed bylaw amendment that would make the homeowner responsible for any action taken by the association *against* the homeowner. As if this weren't bad enough, the phrase was further modified to read, "The homeowner must pay all reasonable attorney fees of *not less* than $1,000." Since when is it reasonable to require a homeowner to pay $1,000 no matter how little work an attorney has done? This practice led MHA to refer to such bylaw rewrites as *predatory bylaw revisions*. You can find other examples on the MHA website. The moral of the story is this: NEVER sign a bylaw revision that you do not completely understand.

As a first step to amending bylaws, a committee of homeowners should go over the existing bylaws and determine what sections need to be changed and why. This committee should be prepared to explain to the rest of the community why this change is needed. To save money, it is wise to send out a draft of the changes to the community for comment before engaging an attorney. Once the community is comfortable with the changes, the board hires an attorney to properly format and word the new bylaw language and make sure it does not contradict any existing laws.

As with rule changes, the bylaws of an association may not be amended without specific numbers of affirmative votes in proportion to the overall community size. MCA 11-103.1 and 104(e) state: "Unless a higher percentage is required in the Bylaws, the Bylaws may be amended by the affirmative vote of unit owners having at least 66⅔ percent of the votes in the council of unit owners."

Unfortunately, there is no similar section in the Maryland Homeowners Association Act. Therefore, it's especially important to know what your association's governing documents state as the percentage needed to change bylaws. This number can be as small as the majority of owners that attend the amendment meeting. In a recent case in Columbia, Maryland, an HOA's bylaws were amended with only 19 percent of the homeowners approving the amendment. In another case in

Gaithersburg, Maryland, when a homeowner brought a suit against her HOA claiming that the governing body had no right to fine her for an alleged offense, the judge ruled that the percentage of homeowners who had approved the bylaw amendment allowing fines in the first place was too small to represent the will of the community, and so he threw the amendment out entirely.

Homeowners may want to work with their HOAs to amend their governing documents to match the MCA's 66⅔ percent vote requirement to prevent a small majority of homeowners from changing bylaws and forcing their will on the rest of the community. Associations would do well to amend only limited sections at a time so that all the homeowners understand exactly what is being changed.

The Maryland Homeowners Association recommends that you follow these guidelines if you are participating in a bylaws amendment process for your association:

1. Be sure that you or whoever is responsible for drafting the communications to your neighbors thoroughly explains the rationale for the bylaw change in writing. This could be someone from the bylaw amendment committee, your manager, or someone from the board. This written rationale should not be in "legalese" but in easy-to-understand language and should be distributed to every homeowner.

2. When sending your suggested amendments, place the exact language of the amendment within the text of the existing bylaws so that the changes stand out. It's common to put the amendment language in **bold** and put the text being altered or deleted in [brackets].

How Rules Are Made and Changed

As mentioned earlier, bylaw amendments are approved by a specified number of affirmative votes of the community at a meeting called for this purpose. Homeowners usually may be present in person or by a signed proxy ballot. Some boards say their community is too "apathetic" to even return amendment proxies. Usually this happens when difficult-to-understand amendment text is sent out without a careful explanation of why the amendment is needed and what the text means. This can be avoided by making the effort to be understandable.

CHAPTER 4

Resolving Disputes

E ven though we hope that clear rules and regulations and reasonable neighbors will lead to a peaceful community, conflicts do arise when there is a difference of opinion. The association's board has no power to deal with neighbor-neighbor conflicts. However, the board is required to enforce the covenants in the bylaws and in the rules and regulations. Fortunately, MCA 11-113's dispute resolution mechanism protects every unit owner's right to a fair hearing. Surprisingly, the Maryland Homeowners Association Act has no formal dispute resolution mechanism, although a bill to do just that has been introduced repeatedly in the Maryland legislature. To be safe, most savvy attorneys recommend that their HOA clients follow the Maryland Condominium Act when handling disputes and imposing sanctions.

So what does the MCA proscribe? Many governing documents give your association the right to impose penalties for bylaw or rule violations. However, MCA 11-113 protects the unit owner's right to a fair hearing before any penalties can be imposed. A board may not impose a fine, suspend voting privileges, or take away any privileges until the unit owner in question has a chance to defend himself in a hearing called for that purpose. The hearing is usually before the board in an executive session, that is, in a closed meeting of the board and the unit owner in question. The required process is as follows:

1. An official letter must be sent to the unit owner describing the alleged violation, the action needed to correct the violation, and the period within which the violation must be corrected. This period must give the unit owner at least ten days.

2. If the violation continues, the board must serve the violator with a written notice of a hearing to be held by the board, or a committee nominated by the board for this purpose. The hearing is closed to the community and the minutes of this meeting are not released to the other homeowners. The hearing notice must contain the nature of the alleged violation, the action required to correct the violation, the time and place of the hearing, and an invitation for the alleged violator to attend the hearing. At this hearing, the alleged violator should produce any statement, evidence, or witnesses on his or her behalf.

If you've been accused unjustly of violating the bylaws or other governing documents of your association, the hearing is the time for you to prove your innocence. Often, a person who knows he or she is in violation will choose not to attend the hearing. When this happens, the person's absence must be recorded in yet another letter to him or her. If the individual attends the hearing, the session is held and the results, including any sanctions imposed, must be written up and sent to the alleged violator. The results of the hearing must also be included in the minutes of the executive session. If the alleged violator does not agree with the results of the hearing, he or she may appeal the decision to the courts of Maryland.

Many association bylaws allow the association to levy reasonable fines on a homeowner in violation of its rules and regulations. MCA 11-109(d)(16) also allows reasonable fines for uncorrected violations. Fines are a way to encourage compliance with the association's declaration, bylaws, and rules and regulations. However, fines are not intended to be a source of income for the association and should be used only when all else fails. Many other sanctions can be used to encourage someone to comply with rules, such as withholding access to amenities like swimming pools or tennis courts, but only if the bylaws allow such sanctions. Most bylaws say fines must be "reasonable." The MHAA does not address fines and so the homeowner association's governing documents would prevail.

If a homeowner still fails to comply, that homeowner can be sued by the association or any other homeowner for damages. The winning party in such a suit is entitled to an award for legal fees if the court so decides. Alternatively, if the violation in question is a failure to pay assessment fees, the association may choose to put a lien on the owner's condo or home, and possibly foreclose. If you were unfortunate enough to have a lien put on your property because of a rule violation, it would be wise for you to hire an attorney to help you get it removed.

Of course, it is far better to continue to try to work out some sort of agreement rather than settling the problem in court. The Maryland Mediation and Conflict Resolution Office (MACRO) of the Maryland Courts (see the Resources section at the end of this book for contact information) will help you find a mediator. Mediation is a neutral process in which boards and homeowners are able to have a facilitated conversation about the dispute. This process helps both sides "be reasonable."

The Contract Lien Act

Probably the most powerful tool an association has to make sure that you pay your monthly assessments is the ability to create a lien on your home and potentially foreclose on this lien. You agreed to this possibility when you bought your home and agreed to all the provisions in your association's governing documents.

Real estate liens attach to the property and do not follow the debtor when he or she transfers ownership to someone else. The lien will show up in a title search and most mortgage companies will not approve a mortgage for a home with a lien on it. If you have had a lien placed on your home because of unpaid assessments, ask your manager for a copy of your payment history. Are you being billed for something you already paid? In 2013, a woman in Olney, Maryland, sued her HOA's management company for placing a lien on her home for a $236 fee she had paid two years earlier. She won her case and was awarded $25,000 in damages by the jury.

If your lien was placed for a valid debt that you have repaid, make sure you get a certificate of release from the association. You can also check your county's land records electronically to make sure the lien's release has been recorded. See the Resources section at the end of this book for information on how to electronically access Maryland land records through MDLANDREC.

If you are in financial trouble, inform your board of directors and try to work out a temporary payment plan (in writing) with them. Don't just stop paying. Ten years ago in Maryland, a family was foreclosed on and thrown out of their home for being a mere $25 in arrears.

Since almost no one reads that package of paper they are given when they consider buying a home in a condo or HOA, most people find out about what they have agreed to the hard way. Fortunately, Maryland passed legislation in 2007 to create the Maryland Foreclosure Prevention Service. This service provides foreclosure prevention resources to homeowners. Maryland's reputation as a "rocket docket" state, in which families could lose their home in days, has been replaced by a required mediation process and longer time frame for foreclosure. See the Resources section at the end of this book for contact information for the Foreclosure Prevention Service.

In the past, you could also lose your home because of unpaid fines or unpaid attorney fees. Since assessing "fines" is not a perfect art and attorney fees can be inflated artificially, the Maryland legislature passed a law in 2013 (Real Property, chapter 14-204) specifying restrictions on when a home can be foreclosed. The new law states that an association can foreclose on a lien if the damages secured by the lien consist solely of delinquent periodic assessments or special assessments and/or *reasonable* costs or attorney fees directly related to the filing of the lien. In the latter case, the attorney fees may not exceed the amount of the delinquent assessments. Also, since imposing fines is a subjective decision, a foreclosure action may not include fines imposed by the governing body or attorney fees related to the recovering the fines. For example, if a homeowner is being fined for something as simple as not cutting his grass, should this be the basis for a foreclosure? Clearly not.

This MHA-supported legislation was a step forward in protecting homeowners from predatory foreclosures. But you should be warned that none of this makes skipping your assessment fees a good idea. Some homeowners believe they are justified in not paying their assessment if the association fails to provide services. In fact, nothing in Maryland law allows you to withhold payment of assessments regardless of the reason. In a recent case, an elderly woman in Utah thought that since she did not use the HOA's amenities, she didn't have to pay her monthly assessment fee. She said she never received warning letters and lost her paid-for home to foreclosure. She now pays $900 a month rent to the new owner to live in what was formerly her house.

Consumer Protection

The board of directors must make sure it follows federal, state, and local laws in all areas of its operation. Ignorance of the law is never an acceptable excuse for violations. I hope that this book gives conscientious board members enough information so that they will keep to the straight and narrow when conducting their duties.

Violations of the MCA and the MHAA are within the scope of the enforcement duties of the Maryland attorney general's Consumer Protection Division (CPD) (MCA 11-130 and MHAA 11B-115). If you believe your board is in violation of the law or otherwise acting in a way that conflicts with the law, I encourage you to first discuss the situation with your board or a board representative and give them an opportunity to correct the situation. It's especially helpful if you give the board a copy of the statute that covers the specific situation with which you are concerned. Unless they've taken relevant courses or done extensive reading on their own, most board members rely on the advice of their association manager. So naturally, that advice is only as good as the knowledge of the manager. Managers are human. Now that you have this book, you can help your manager by pointing out errors and steering him or her to the relevant sections in Maryland law.

If, after trying to persuade your board to do otherwise, they haven't corrected their violation of the law, you can report the situation to the CPD (see the Resources section at the end of this book for contact information). The CPD will contact your board and ask them to comment on your complaint. If the board is in the wrong, the CPD will send a letter to the board explaining the pertinent law and how the matter should be resolved. On some occasions, the CPD will take legal action against a board if the situation is not resolved.

Note that the CPD deals only with violations of Maryland law and not violations of an association's governing documents such as the declaration, bylaws, covenants, or rules and regulations. To seek enforcement of the governing documents, you should first explain to the board, first at a board meeting and then by letter, why a particular association bylaw or rule should be enforced. If the board still does not enforce the rule and mediation is not an option, you have the option of suing the association and incurring all the costs involved in litigation. Should you decide a lawsuit is your only option, try to get other homeowners who share your concerns to help with the legal costs. Of course, if you win, the court can choose to make your association responsible for all reasonable legal fees. However, lawsuits are disruptive for a community and should be used only as a last resort.

In addition to the CPD, some Maryland counties offer dispute resolution help and advice for homeowners and their boards. Contact information for these offices are listed in the Resources section at the end of this book.

If working directly with your board doesn't work, and you can't get satisfaction from your county (or if your county is part of the problem), you can also file some types of complaints with the federal government. A newly formed federal agency, the Consumer Financial Protection Bureau, wants to hear about possible financial fraud in HOA and condominium associations. Contact information is in the Resources section at the end of this book.

CHAPTER 5

How Information Should Get Around

As mentioned earlier, common ownership communities (COCs) are really small businesses. An incorporated COC must follow Maryland corporate law (Corporations and Associations Article in the Maryland Code, mainly Sections 2-401 through 2-419 and Sections 2-501 through 5-206, among others) but the MCA and the MHAA govern many aspects of how the community is run. For example, corporation law is set up to protect the trade secrets and other interests of a corporation, and many board actions can be done in closed meetings out of view of the membership.

The Maryland General Assembly recognized that this is not the way owners of homes in condominiums and homeowners associations in Maryland wanted to live, and so it enacted the MCA and the MHAA to protect the rights of homeowners.

Annual Meeting

At regular board meetings, the board may limit topics to those on the agenda so the board can conduct required business in a timely manner. However, since the MCA and the MHAA state that there must be time allotted at *every* regular board meeting for homeowner comments, such a time period must be on the meeting agenda. If many people in attendance wish to comment, the board may limit the speaking time for homeowners. It's become common to limit speaking time to three minutes. The board is not required to answer at that point. Any board would be wise to investigate whatever issue has been brought up and either respond directly to the individual or put the issue on the next board meeting's agenda for more public discussion.

In addition to these meetings, both the MCA and the MHAA require associations to hold at least one meeting each year, the annual meeting, at which the agenda is open to any matter related to the condominium (MCA 11-109(c)(7)(iv) and MHAA 11B-111(3) (iv)). This annual meeting is different from regular board meetings. Operationally, this is the one meeting where owners may bring up for discussion any topic relative to the governing of the association.

Because the annual meeting is usually well attended, many communities use the annual meeting for board elections as well. However, the election is secondary to the primary purpose of the annual meeting, which is to allow an orderly open discussion between unit owners. The board president is responsible for controlling the meeting so that no one person dominates the discussion.

Distribution: Written Information or Materials

In between meetings, you or your board may wish to share information with community members. Maryland law protects your right as a homeowner to distribute information related to your condominium association or homeowner association to the rest of your community. MCA 11-111.3 and MHAA 11B-111.3 say that an association may not restrict a unit owner from distributing any information or materials regarding the operation of the association if that unit owner uses the same distribution means as the association. For example:

1. If your association distributes information door-to-door, any homeowner may distribute information relative to the association door-to-door.
2. If your association provides information on a website, any homeowner may also provide information and opinions on a private website. Of course, the homeowner must have a disclaimer that makes clear that the opinions presented are private opinions and not those of the association.
3. If your association sends out information by mail or e-mail, any unit owner may send information related to the association to the entire community by mail or e-mail.

Since mailing lists are considered community association records, and as we've already learned in Chapter 2, all owners are entitled to copies of association records, you may also request a copy of the mailing list at any time. However, the mailing list or any of the distribution means described here *may not be used for commercial advertising or other personal uses*. It can be used only for discussing association matters. You are also responsible for any charges incurred if you choose to communicate with your neighbors en masse, but if the issue is important, it becomes a small price to pay. Thus, freedom of speech is alive and well in Maryland condominium and HOA communities.

Of course, an association forum on the Internet, such a Google or Yahoo group or an e-mail discussion list, maintained by the association, is a wonderful way to provide information and encourage civil discussion between neighbors. With an online forum, any homeowner can make his or her opinion known to the community and the board can quickly get information out to the community. However, the etiquette rules for posting must be clearly stated. If a homeowner uses the system to abuse others, that homeowner should be removed from the forum immediately. Any association online forum should have a board member as an administrator, since an association can be sued for posting inappropriate material.

Even through there is a risk to forming an association online forum, the goodwill generated in the community is worth it.

CHAPTER 6

Electing Your Board of Directors

A common ownership community is built on the concept that homeowners are willing to give a portion of their time to help govern the association. Serving on the board of directors is a shared responsibility and at some point, everyone should volunteer to do it, because serving on the board gives owners an appreciation of the effort needed to keep a community functioning well. If you have ideas for making the community a better place, then get elected to the board and make it happen. Hopefully, *Happy Homes* will help new Maryland board members understand what is needed to do the job well.

Board Elections

The Maryland Condominium Act guides the process for condominium board elections. The Maryland Homeowners Association Act does not address the conduct of HOA elections, but HOA boards would be wise to follow the legal procedure described for condominium associations.

MCA 11-109(c)(13) states that:

1. A letter asking for nominations must be sent to the community forty-five days before the date of the election. This letter should state the number of board vacancies and have a nomination form that the candidate can fill in and mail back.

2. Unless otherwise provided in the association bylaws, any unit owner may nominate himself or herself or any other unit owner to be a member of the board of directors. To run for the board, a candidate must be an association member in "good standing," which means not having a lien on your home for nonpayment of assessments. Some association bylaws give other sanctions that would cause a homeowner to not be in good standing.

3. Candidates nominated by others should then be asked if they are willing to serve. All candidates who indicate a willingness to serve must be listed on the election ballot. The board of directors is responsible for ensuring that proper procedures are followed.

4. Candidates must be listed on the ballot in alphabetical order with no indication of preference. Election materials such as candidate statements and bios prepared by the association must be presented in the same way and not indicate any preference.

5. Nominations from the floor at the election meeting are allowed under the MCA, but anyone serious about running for the board should be sure to be listed on the ballot since proxy ballots (discussed shortly) are submitted before the election meeting and the numbers

could be against you if you are nominated from the floor. Much as for an election for public office, all candidates should distribute to the community a summary of their positions and why they should be elected to the board of directors. Unless stated differently in the association's bylaws, individuals running for the board of directors are elected by a majority of the votes of the unit owners present at the election meeting either in person or by proxy. (See MCA 11-109(c)(15).)

Electronic Notices

The original Maryland Condominium Act dates back at least twenty-five years, well before the electronic delivery of information became the norm. Because of this, the MCA and the MHAA originally specified that association notices must be delivered by U.S. mail or by hand delivery. To allow associations to take advantage of the speed and low cost of digital communication, the MCA and the MHAA were amended several years ago to allow e-mail voting, but only with the permission of the unit owner (MCA 11-139.1 and 11-139.2.) The same requirements are in MHAA 11B-113.2.

Thus, an association may provide notice of meetings and deliver information by electronic means if the owner gives the association *prior written authorization to do so and an officer of the board certifies in writing that the association has provided information by e-mail to the owner.* If an owner does not give prior written authorization to receive association information electronically, all information must be mailed or hand delivered to that owner. Moreover, if the manager finds that the association is unable to deliver two consecutive electronic notices, then the use of electronic delivery is terminated and U.S. mail must be used to send all formal communications.

The acts also allow the electronic transmission of election votes or proxies if the electronic transmission contains information that verifies that the vote or proxy is authentic. Verifying authenticity presents a technical challenge. If anonymous voting is required and the anonymity of the electronic vote cannot be guaranteed, then owners must be given the option of casting anonymous printed ballots.

Voting—Quorum and Proxies

In order for an election or other vote of the association to be valid, there must be a "quorum" of the members participating. The MCA states that unless the bylaws provide otherwise, a quorum is deemed present if 25 percent of the total number of votes are cast either in person or by proxy. Proxy votes are allowed so that votes can be cast without the voter being present. In a *directed proxy*, homeowners indicate the candidate they want to select or whether they agree with a proposal that is up for a vote. *Nondirected proxies* can be used only to reach a quorum or vote on a proposed action, not for the election of a board member. These votes are tallied at the election meeting and are valid for quorum purposes and the election of the board. Proxy votes are tallied at the election meeting along with votes cast in person.

When homeowners do not return their proxy ballots, the community may have difficulty making a quorum, and without a quorum the election will not be valid. If there is no quorum, another election meeting must be called. Since repeat meetings cost the association money, every responsible homeowner should return his or her proxy or vote in person. It is an important part of being a good homeowner-citizen. Plus, if there has to be a second election mailing and meeting, the extra cost will be borne by every homeowner. If an association is unable to elect enough people to the board to meet its quorum of directors, the community could find itself in receivership (discussed later). The required composition of a board is dictated by the association's bylaws. Usually, every board has a president, vice president, secretary, and treasurer who are the officers of the association. Others elected to the board would be "at-large" members.

Replacement of Board Members or Officers

The community usually elects homeowners to the board, and it is the elected board that appoints board members to the officer positions. Unfortunately, some individuals, given a position of authority, seem to go a little bit nuts. Others may shirk their responsibilities once elected. If you've been stuck with such an individual on your board, you have no choice but to remove him or her. Further, if a board of directors is not following either its own governing documents or Maryland state law and members are making no effort to educate themselves in the requirements of the law, owners may have no choice but to replace some or all of the board members. Most bylaws specify that removal and replacement of board members can be done only by a majority vote of the membership at a special membership meeting called for that purpose. A less disruptive approach is to elect new directors over time as terms of office end.

A board of directors can remove an officer from his or her position as an officer, but that removed officer remains a member of the board. A majority of the members of the board can remove an individual from an officer position, but only a majority vote of the homeowners can remove an individual from the board.

Appointment of a Receiver

During my tenure, the Maryland Homeowners Association had a call from an HOA owner saying that their HOA had been "defunct" for more than three years and that no one had been paying HOA fees. There had been no board elections, but one person, who used to be the president, had been trying to keep the association from completely falling apart by hiring landscaping crews himself. That wasn't working well, so the past president had recently hired an attorney to try to get things back on track. Together, the past president and the attorney sent a letter to the community with an announcement of an upcoming board election as well as a notice that all homeowners owed the association $1,800 for past dues.

A number of things were wrong with this situation, not the least of which was that the president has no legal right to act alone. If this community's bylaws require a five-person board, then it takes a majority of board members (at least three) to conduct any business on the association's behalf. Despite his good intentions, everything that this past president had signed for the past three years was unenforceable. Moreover, the poor fellow could have been personally responsible for any payments he improperly authorized.

Maryland law states that if a board fails to fill vacancies on the board of directors to constitute a quorum, three or more homeowners may petition the circuit court to appoint a receiver to manage the association (MHAA 11B-111.5; MCA 11-109.3). If no one petitions the court, the community is likely to fall into bankruptcy. Once the association is stable again, the receiver can arrange for the election of a board of directors.

The court usually appoints an attorney to be the receiver, and attorneys do not come cheap. Having a receiver is an expensive solution to something that should never be allowed to happen.

Unfortunately, some situations, such as the impending bankruptcy of the association, are impossible to remedy without a receiver. If the board lacks a quorum, the process to be followed when asking for a receiver is as follows:

1. At least thirty days before petitioning the court, the group of owners shall mail to the existing board, if there is one, a notice describing the petition and the proposed action.
2. The owners must post a copy of the notice in a conspicuous place or send it to every owner.
3. If the board does not fill the vacancies within the thirty-day period, the group may proceed with the petition to the court.

To be appointed, a receiver may not own a unit in the condominium or a home in the community; the receiver shall have all the powers and duties of the board and shall serve until a quorum of board members is elected. The salary of the receiver, court costs, and reasonable attorney fees are common expenses of the association.

The moral of this story is that without the participation of the entire community, the association is at risk. You should volunteer to serve on the board so that your association *never* has to appoint a receiver.

CHAPTER 7

Your Association and Your Money

When you bought into your common ownership community, you purchased not only a part of the assets of the association but a part of the association's liabilities as well. Every month (or perhaps yearly) you pay a fee to your association, which represents your share of the association's bills. The association uses this money to maintain common property, to pay condo or HOA insurance and management fees, and for many other things.

Some associations are self-managed and the treasurer collects assessments and pays bills. More often, though, associations use a professional management company to handle finances for the community. Though this decision itself incurs an additional expense, it's well worth it—the amount of knowledge needed to manage what is, in essence, a small corporation, is vast and frankly best handled by professionals. Unfortunately, going this route can open the door to possible problems. In my time with the Maryland Homeowners

Association, I learned of several situations in which bank statements were electronically manipulated by a manager and then sent on to the association. Board presidents and treasurers have also embezzled money from association accounts.

Every individual on the board of directors has the responsibility to protect association funds, not just the treasurer. To strengthen good governance in your community, the MHA recommends that your board put in place a number of best practices designed to provide greater administrative transparency and accountability over daily operations.

Safeguarding Association Funds

When such services are contracted via a management company, the board remains the corporate entity that is ultimately held responsible for fraud associated with fiscal mismanagement, accounting lapses, and poor bookkeeping. In some cases in Maryland, either an individual manager has embezzled association funds or a management company has gone out of business, taking the association's reserve funds with them. This is why you have fidelity insurance (we'll talk more about this in Chapter 8), and you'll probably get your money back, but only after a very painful legal process. To avoid this, board members should be diligent and incorporate good financial safeguards.

First, a responsible board should always require dual signatures for any expenditure of condominium funds, presumably the signatures of a manager and a board member. No one person should have sole control of association funds. If cosigning checks is inconvenient, one or more board members should have electronic read-only access to all association accounts. Since most banks offer images of the checks written and cashed to account holders, it should be regular practice for a board member to review these checks electronically and compare them against the figures in the board's monthly reports.

Second, if your association hires a manager to deal with finances, the board can have the bank send a duplicate monthly statement directly to the board treasurer. Again, the treasurer should compare the bank's figures against those in the monthly report received from the management company. If the management company is willing to provide the treasurer with copies of any checks written from the association account, this information along with a directly mailed bank statement can substitute for read-only access.

It's hard to believe that a neighbor or professional manager would steal association funds, but it does happen. There's no need to be paranoid and try to keep everything in house or overly complicated, however. Installing these simple safeguards will go a very long way toward the financial stability and safety of your community.

Annual Budget Meeting

By law, each year the association's proposed budget for the following year must be sent to all owners for written comment and a budget meeting scheduled for oral comment. The MCA and the MHAA are very specific as to the budgeted items the proposed budget must include (see MCA 11-109.2(b) and MHAA 11B-112.2). These required items are income, administration, maintenance, utilities, general expenses, reserves, and capital items. Since this part of the laws was written many years ago and is somewhat out of date, a proposed budget usually has other categories as well. This is okay, as long as the legally required items are incorporated in the budget.

The proposed budget must be sent to owners by the management company thirty days before an open meeting is called to adopt the budget. Owners are encouraged to provide written comments to the board as well as comment at this open meeting. If an owner suggests a change, the board can vote, in open session, on whether to include the change in a modified budget. Once all changes have been made, the board votes to adopt the modified budget and it becomes the budget for the following year. You and your board, however, must be aware of the voting rules as stated in your association's governing documents and follow those rules. Some associations, for example, require that *all* unit owners must vote on a proposed budget as opposed to the usual quorum.

Sometimes, because of increasing costs or unexpected circumstances, an association may need to adjust the budget during the year. If it becomes necessary to increase a budgeted amount more than 15 percent, the board may adopt an amendment to the budget. This must occur at another open meeting with the owners. Again, it's important to check in with your association's governing documents as to the rules. In some communities, owners must vote to approve this increase, while in others only the board needs to approve the modified budget.

Regardless of who needs to vote, the meeting procedure remains the same. The board must send a notice of the budget amendment meeting to owners at least ten days before the meeting is held. In this notice, it's best if the reasons for increasing the budget increase are carefully explained. Again, the board (or membership, as per your association's governing documents) votes at an open meeting to accept the amended budget.

Special Assessments

The law gives no guidance in its budget process on how to implement a special assessment. A special assessment is levied when some unforeseen event has occurred such that more money is needed to pay a bill. A good example of such an event is a monster snowstorm that requires more snow removal money than the association previously budgeted. When the budget is amended, the money still needs to come from somewhere—from the community members, usually, which then results in a special assessment. Typically, only the board votes to implement a special assessment. However, some association bylaws state that special assessments can be passed only by a majority vote of the entire membership. As always, be sure to check your governing documents.

Special assessments are disruptive to the budgets of most homeowners and therefore should be used only when there is an emergency expense. The board should make every effort to predict upcoming expenses and adjust the annual assessment accordingly.

Financial Audits

In earlier chapters, we discussed the fact that the law allows any unit or homeowner access to most books and records of their association. Further, the MCA requires that the board keep books and records in accordance with good accounting practices. The MHAA has no similar requirement, but, as mentioned before, savvy HOA attorneys recommend that all HOAs follow the more stringent provisions of the MCA.

As a best practice, boards should have association books and records audited yearly. An audit should reveal if any funds are missing. I recommend using an independent certified public accountant (CPA) to conduct this audit, and that the association board—rather than the management company—choose the CPA. Additionally, I recommend that the CPA send his or her audit directly to the board as well as to the management company.

All unit owners are entitled to review the audit report. A review of the audit report and the monthly financial reports provides information to unit owners about the financial health of the association.

If your association is not conducting yearly audits as a matter of course, you can request one. MCA 11-116(b) states that unit owners representing only 5 percent of the units can request an audit. Thus, in an association with 100 units, the owners of five of the units can request an audit. Only one audit for every twelve-month period can be requested. The request should be in writing, addressed to the board, and signed by each of the requesting unit owners. Once the request is made, the board *must* have the audit done. The law further states that the cost of the audit is a common expense. There is no comparable text in the MHAA, but, again, most attorneys would recommend that the homeowners association follow the MCA rules.

CHAPTER 8

Understanding Insurance and Who's Liable

Many fine books are available that explain the ownership difference between a condominium and a homeowners association, so I don't want to go too deeply into this subject. However, one cannot discuss insurance without an understanding of this difference. In Maryland law, you'll see that the owner of a condominium is called a "unit owner" and the owner of a home in an HOA is called a "lot owner."

In an HOA, even town house HOAs, each owner owns the lot that the house is on and usually the entire house itself. In a condo, each owner owns a share of the common elements of the condominium association. Usually, only the air space between the condominium's four walls is reserved for the owner's private use. Since you own a portion of the entire association's assets and a portion of the association's liabilities, insurance coverage is necessary to preserve your assets and minimize your liabilities. Sometimes, the association's insurance policy will cover parts of the community that you do not use. For example, if there are ten town house buildings in your association and two of the buildings are in a flood zone, paying for the flood insurance is an expense borne by all the condominium owners, not just those who live in the flood zone.

In a condo, only the condominium association can buy hazard insurance for all the buildings, whereas in an HOA, usually each owner can purchase insurance for his or her home. However, governing documents do vary as to who is responsible for purchasing insurance, so you must check your documents for guidance as to who pays for what.

Property Insurance

The insurance policy of most condominium associations, paid for out of assessments, covers the association's common property and individual units "***exclusive of improvements and betterments installed in units by unit owners other than the developer***" (MCA 11-114). As an example of what "improvements and betterments" means, if your building is fifteen years old and you still have the original kitchen cabinets, damage to these cabinets will be covered by the condominium association's master policy. However, if you have *replaced* the kitchen cabinets, the insurance payer will be your private homeowner's condo owner policy (I'll explain this in a moment), not the association's policy.

Usually, in the event of a claim your manager will notify both insurance companies and the companies will work out who pays what, but it's important that you understand your rights and responsibilities in these situations. (Remember my story from the Introduction?) Always notify your association manager before you notify the insurance companies. It is sometimes more economical for the association to pay for any damage itself than to have insurance premiums increase because of too many claims.

I encourage all owners to regularly examine their association's master policy or a summary of the master policy to determine what constitutes a "covered loss." For example, fire and wind are usually considered a covered loss but flood is not, which is why separate flood insurance is advisable if the association lies in a floodplain. You can request the paperwork at any time—associations are required by law to make their insurance policies available for owner inspection. Further, Maryland law states that a notice of insurance coverage must go to every homeowner yearly.

Individual Unit Owner's Policy

Improvements to the unit that are made by a current or prior unit owner must by insured by a second homeowner policy for which the unit owner pays the premiums. This policy also covers the owner's personal belongings within a unit. Every condominium or homeowner should have an individual policy. If you rent out your condominium, you should insist that your tenant carry "renter's insurance" to protect the tenant's personal belongings.

In the case of damage to multiple units, Maryland law states that the unit owner in whose unit the damage started is responsible for the deductible, which can be up to $5,000 per occurrence. If the damage is below the amount of the deductible, the unit owner should not bother filing an insurance claim.

For a small extra fee, the owner can have the association insurance deductible expense be part of the coverage provided by the homeowner's policy. For another small fee, the home-owner's policy can also cover individual unit owners against a monetary judgment against the condominium association that might be in excess of what is covered by the association's liability insurance. If an accident happens on association property and the association is found liable, judgments can be in the millions of dollars. Since a judgment is a "common expense," each homeowner would be responsible for paying his or her share. Just spending a few dollars more can protect you against this financial burden.

The MHAA does not require a specific type or amount of homeowner insurance coverage. Typically, this information can be found in the HOA's bylaws. However, a prudent HOA home-owner would be wise to follow the advice of an insurance profes-sional who is familiar with HOAs and can recommend individual insurance coverage that is compatible with that of the HOA.

One last thing you should know about property insurance: MCA 11-112 is labeled "Eminent Domain." This does not refer to the government taking your property, which is dealt with in Title 12 of the Maryland Real Property Code. MCA 11-112 refers to the association taking ownership of a property during a pending or threatened condemnation proceeding. An example would be a catastrophic fire that destroys a block of homes so badly that the insurance company deems it is not worthwhile to rebuild them. Although eminent domain is often explained in governing documents, this section describes how the insurance proceeds will be distributed among the unit owners.

Fidelity Insurance

In addition to protecting your property, it's wise to protect your association. Fidelity insurance is a type of insurance designed to protect an association from losses caused by the dishonest acts of its board or management company. I've known of sad circumstances in which association managers and even board members have embezzled association funds. In a recent case, because of accusations of embezzlement, an entire management company had to shut down, taking millions of dollars in reserve funds with them.

Fidelity insurance allows associations to recover stolen funds. By law, umbrella policies must include fidelity insurance. MCA 11-114.1 and MHAA 11B-111.6 describe whom fidelity insurance must cover, how much coverage an association must carry, and who pays for it. The fidelity insurance required provides for the indemnification of the association and its members against loss resulting from acts or omissions arising from fraud, dishonesty, or criminal acts by any officer, director, managing agent, or anyone else who controls and disperses association funds. As with property insurance, a copy of the fidelity insurance policy must be made available for any owner to review. The MCA and the MHAA require the following:

1. That the amount of fidelity insurance must be the lesser of three months' worth of annual assessments plus the total amount held in reserve accounts *or* $3,000,000, and
2. That the association is responsible for purchasing this insurance.

CHAPTER 9

Making Changes to Your Home

Conventional wisdom tells us that some uniformity of design in a community, especially if homes are glued together as in townhomes, enhances the beauty of a community and adds to the value of each home. Thus, before you launch a project that alters the exterior of your home, you should consult the architectural guidelines in your association's governing documents. Before starting work you will probably need to submit an architectural modification application to your board that clearly states what kind of improvement you want to make, what materials will be used, and the color of the improvement. Many consider this step a nuisance, but it really is there to save you the cost of having to redo a project because of using the wrong color or materials. Getting preapproval for changes should be considered an insurance policy on your investment in an alteration.

Improvements, Alterations, or Additions

Once you submit your application for improvements, alterations, or additions, it will be considered and hopefully approved by the board or by the association's architectural committee. Once it is approved, you can start work.

Such rules need not result in communities or homes that look totally alike. Each community can make its architectural guidelines as stringent or as liberal as the members want. Architectural guidelines are a type of "rule" and when introduced must follow the process (described in Chapter 3) for rule making. Thus, the entire community has the opportunity to comment on or change proposed guidelines.

For example, some town house governing documents specify that the association plants and maintains all front and rear gardens, whereas other associations allow homeowners the freedom to be creative and maintain individualized gardens (so long as the garden is well maintained and doesn't become a jungle, of course).

Your community should decide what it wants its overall look to be. Total uniformity does not have to be the norm. If your bylaws currently state that the association controls all plantings and you want some uniqueness in your community, gather the support of your neighbors and amend the bylaws to allow individuality.

The Maryland Condominium Act weighs in on unit owner alterations only as they relate to the structural integrity of the condominium building. (See MCA 11-115(1).) If you live in a multilevel condominium, it should be clear that you shouldn't do anything that might make the building fall down. If you are foolish enough to do something like that, not only will you face the wrath of your neighbors but also you will have violated the MCA.

Making Changes to Your Home

The Maryland Homeowners Association Act is silent on improvements, alterations, or additions, so owners in HOA communities should refer to their governing documents. These documents usually have a similar approval process to MCA 11-115, which states that subject to the provisions in your declaration or bylaws and other provisions of law such as county law, a unit owner:

1. May, subject to association approval, make any improvement or alteration to his or her unit that does not impair the structural integrity or mechanical systems or lessen the support of any portion of the condominium.
2. May not alter, make additions to, or change the appearance of the common elements or the exterior appearance of a unit or other portion of the condominium, without permission of the council of unit owners.
3. After acquiring an adjoining unit or an adjoining part of an adjoining unit, may, subject to association approval, remove or alter any intervening partition, even if the partition in whole or in part is a common element, if those acts do not impair the structural integrity or mechanical systems or lessen the support of any portion of the condominium. (However, the board shall give prior approval and an amendment to the declaration and plat(s) shall be filed among the land records of the county in which the condominium is located under the name of the condominium.) Removal of partitions or creation of apertures (any opening left in a wall for a door, window, or for ventilation) is not an alteration of boundaries.

Clearly, moving condominium walls is not for the faint of heart. Again, I realize all of this can seem like unnecessary hoops to jump through, but try to keep in mind what could happen without such protections in place. Moreover, as annoying as the process may seem, please don't try to sidestep the approval process thinking that no one will know you've made an interior alteration or that you'd rather wait and see if you get a letter. This kind of behavior simply isn't neighborly, and more importantly, it might come back to haunt you.

Hiring Contractors

I highly recommend that, as a matter of course, an owner or board looking to hire a contractor for exterior or interior work get three bids for any contract. Don't automatically use the individuals that work for your management company. Remember, your management company must keep their hired workers active or the company loses money, so their motivations may not be entirely pure. There's no harm, however, in having your management company bid on a project along with other contractors when work is needed on common elements; just be sure that all sealed bids go to one of the board members rather than the manager.

Before selecting an individual or company, always ask for copies of licenses, permits, and a copy of a certificate of liability before signing a contract. If the individual or company is reluctant to give you a copy of a license, be wary; the contractor may not have the credentials claimed. You can verify some stated credentials online by visiting the website of the Maryland Department of Labor, Licensing and Regulation. You should also see if there have been complaints against the potential contractor by checking with the Better Business Bureau, the CPD, or your county consumer protection office.

Why go to all this trouble? Let's say, for example, that you are looking for a contractor to maintain the trees on your personal or common property. There are big differences between an arborist (credentialed by the Maryland Arborist Association) and a licensed tree expert (credentialed by the Maryland Department of Natural Resources) and a guy with a chain saw. The person with the lowest bid may not have the experience or credentials to do a good job. See the Resources section at the end of this book for contact information for the Maryland Arborist Association and the Maryland Department of Natural Resources.

In addition to ensuring that the contractor is sufficiently credentialed, ***never allow anyone on your property as a contractor if they don't have liability insurance.*** If the worker docs not have insurance and has an accident, you or your association may be sued for damages.

Here are some additional points to keep in mind before hiring any contactor.

1. Get an estimate in writing that covers labor and materials. Never pay more than one third of the cost as a deposit,[4] and if possible, ask to be billed after all the work is completed. This will give you the leverage to make sure the job is done well before you pay. Read and understand the contract's fine print before signing.
2. Be suspicious of contractors that offer "incentives" or "discounts" to get you to use their company. The contractor will just take the "incentive" money out of the quality of the job.
3. Check references carefully by going to past work sites and looking at the work as well as talking to

---

4 *Maryland law prohibits home improvement contractors from demanding more than one third of the contract price up front. While not required, other service providers should also agree to a deposit of only one third of the total cost. (Maryland Business Regulation Code, Section 8-617.)*

homeowners at that site. If you are having work done on your individual unit or home, speak to board members to see if they are also satisfied with the work.

4. If it is a substantial contract, such as for common buildings, have someone from the company attend a board meeting to respond to questions.

CHAPTER 10

Resale of Your Home or Unit

MCA 11-135 requires that when you sell your condo, you provide certain documents to a prospective buyer fifteen days or more before closing. Usually sellers ask their association's management company to assemble this information, called a *resale package*. This resale package is far more complex than just a photocopy of the association's governing documents. Management companies charge a fee to assemble this package because the information must be up to date and provide information unique to the unit as of that date. For example, if there is a lien on the unit or if there are any pending architectural violations that have not been corrected, that information goes into the resale package. (If you are a buyer, note that while this resale package has important information, it should not take the place of having a licensed building inspector carefully inspect the property.) Similar requirements, as well as some unique ones, are in place for the sale or resale of homes in an HOA. For details, see MHAA 11B-106.

The requirement for a resale package allows condo buyers to be informed about potential problems prior to the sale. Prospective buyers have seven days following delivery of the resale package to cancel their contract. Any deposit money must be returned to the buyer if the contract is canceled.

Documents that must be provided in the resale package are as follows:

1. A copy of the declaration, bylaws, and rules and regulations of the condominium.
2. A statement "disclosing the effect on the proposed conveyance of any right of first refusal or other restraint on the free availability of the unit other than any restraint created by the unit owner."
3. A certificate containing the monthly common expense assessment and any unpaid common expense or special assessment currently due and payable from the selling unit owner.
4. A statement of any other fees payable by the unit owner to the council of unit owners or board of directors.
5. A statement of any pending capital expenditures approved by the board that are not reflected in the current operating budget.
6. The most recent balance sheet and operating budget of the condominium that includes details of the reserve fund.
7. A statement of any judgments against the condominium and the existence of any pending lawsuits involving the condominium association.
8. A statement describing the insurance policies maintained by the association.

9. A statement as to whether the association has knowledge of any alteration or improvement to the unit that violates the unit's limited common elements or any provision of the declaration, bylaws, or rules or regulations.
10. A statement of any violation of health or building codes related to the unit, the limited common elements assigned to the unit, or any other portion of the condominium.
11. A statement as to whether the unit is subject to an extended lease and the provisions governing any extension or renewal of the lease.
12. A description of any recreational or other facilities that are to be used by the unit owners or maintained by them or the council of unit owners (association), and a statement as to whether they are to be part of the common elements.
13. A statement by the unit owner as to whether the unit owner has knowledge of:

    a. Any alteration to the unit or to the limited common elements assigned to the unit that violates any provision of the declaration, bylaws, or rules and regulations; and
    b. Any violation of the health or building codes with respect to the unit or the limited common elements assigned to the unit; and
    c. Whether the unit is subject to an extended lease under state or local law; if so, a copy of the lease must be provided.

There are additional requirements for the resale of a unit in a condominium containing less than seven units. If this applies to you, see MCA 11-135(5)(b).

Anyone who is about to purchase a condo would be wise to carefully review all of the preceding documentation before closing on the sale. Once you close on the deal and become the owner of the unit, all problems associated with the unit transfer to you.

CHAPTER 11

Less Commonly Used Sections of the MCA and the MHAA

All of the preceding chapters have focused on the sections of the MCA and the MHAA that refer to everyday association governance. For completeness, the remaining sections of these acts are briefly discussed in this chapter. Since these situations occur more rarely, I have provided a citation to the section of the appropriate law and a short synopsis of the law. I recommend that the reader go directly to the section of the act cited or consult an association attorney to fully understand these laws

1. **Restrictions on Candidate Signs.** Most condominiums have a section in their governing documents that states that unit owner signs may not be displayed on condominium property. Signs are usually not allowed on the common property, but what about a townhome's

front lawn? An exception to the "no signs" rule is usually made for real estate "For Sale" signs.

This prohibition on signs, however, does not prevent unit owners from displaying candidate support signs during elections for public office. MCA 11-111.2 and MHAA 11B-111.2 protect the right of homeowners to display candidate signs. Note that these laws relate to candidates for public office and not for board elections. Each association may decide whether they want to allow signs for board elections.

These acts state that an association may not prohibit or restrict the display of a candidate sign or a sign that advertises the support or defeat of any particular proposition. The sign may be displayed thirty days before the election and must be removed seven days after the election. The condominium association may restrict the posting of a sign on any common element.

An exception to the "no signs" rule is usually made for real estate "For Sale" signs.

2. **Conversion of Residential Property to Condominiums.** We all know of apartment buildings that have been converted to condominiums. MCA 11-102.1 addresses conversions and attempts to protect all parties involved. If you have received notice from your apartment's owner that your building may be converted into a condominium, you should read this section of the MCA. There is no comparable section in the MHAA.

3. **Termination of Leases.** This should be understood if a conversion of your apartment house to a condominium is planned. See MCA 11-102.2. There is no comparable section in the MHAA.

4. **Condominium Plat.** As described in MCA 11-105, a condominium plat is a diagrammatic plan of the community as certified by a professional surveyor. Each unit of the condominium is designated on the plat. When the declaration and bylaws are recorded, the developer also records the condominium plat at a county land office.

MHAA 11B-112 (c) and 11B-113 describes the information that must be made public in a county homeowners association depository. The HOA depository is separate from the land records. It contains items such as the names of all homeowners associations in each county and the city of Baltimore and the appropriate documents for each association.

Initially, it is the community developer's responsibility to make sure the required documents are filed with the correct county or city agency. Once a board of directors is elected, however, it will be responsible for filing bylaw amendments in the repositories. These bylaw amendments must be recorded in the county depository or land office before they are legal and binding.

5. **Percentage Interests.** MCA 11-107 describes how the association's declaration describes each condominium unit owner's percentage interest in common property. This determines how common expenses and common profits are divided among the owners. In an HOA, the common property percentage responsibility would be part of the disclosure package given to a potential buyer.

6. **Common Expenses and Profits; Assessments; Liens.** MCA 11-110 further clarifies how community expenses and profits are divided among the homeowners in the

community. Most importantly, if you fail to pay your assessments, this section of the MCA is the authority for your association to place a lien on your home for unpaid assessments, late charges, costs of collection, and reasonable attorney fees. Since the further you fall in arrears the more the associated costs go up, a homeowner should give paying association monthly assessments a high priority.

7. **Family Day Care Homes.** MCA 11-111.1 and MHAA 11B-111.1 both describe the steps an individual must take to set up a family day care business in the community. The homeowners in the community have a vote as to whether to allow a day care business to open. The procedure, while elaborate, ensures fairness.

8. **Required Insurance Coverage; Reconstruction.** I hope the reconstruction portion of the MCA never applies to you. This section describes required insurance coverage as well as the actions that must be taken if 80 percent of the unit owners vote not to rebuild. (See MCA 11-114.) There is no analogous section in the MHAA, and the association's governing documents would describe the steps to be taken should reconstruction need to take place.

9. **Mechanics' and Materialmen's Liens.** MCA 11-118 just says that a lien arising as a result of repairs to or improvement of a unit will apply only against the unit and not the association. There is no analogous section in the MHAA.

10. **Warranties.** MCA 11-131 applies only to warranties provided by the developer. MHAA 11B-104 discusses implied warranties briefly.

11. **Disclosure Requirements When Buying a Unit from the Developer.** MCA 11-126 describes the written

disclosures the developer of a new community must give to a prospective buyer. MHAA 11B-105 has similar information. Buyers of homes in HOAs should review disclosures carefully. More and more, developers, not local governments, are responsible for constructing the development's water and sewage systems and roads as well as development amenities. To recoup the cost of this construction, the developer can charge the homeowner a yearly fee for some period of time (often twenty to thirty years). This is a lien that "runs with the land"—that is, the first homeowner pays the fee as long as he or she owns the home. When the home is subsequently sold, the new owner picks up the payments until he or she sells, and so on until the lien period is over. This information may be in the governing documents of the HOA but most often is in amendments that are filed in the land records of the county. The buyers of homes in new developments should therefore affirmatively ask the builder about whether such liens exist, the yearly cost, and the number of years the fee must be paid.

Conclusion

Living in a shared ownership community is very different from either renting a home or owning your lot and home free and clear in a nonassociation community. Every shared ownership community owner commits to following the association's governing documents and all applicable laws when the home is purchased. Moreover and not to be underestimated, shared ownership communities, as I hope I've emphasized sufficiently in this book, operate best when all owners take an active role. The success of any community depends on each owner doing his or her part.

Beyond paying your assessment fees on time, it is essential to the health of an association that every member of the community serve on the board of directors at some point. New board members must become acquainted with the community association's governing documents and all relevant federal, state, and county laws. Ignorance of the law is never an excuse for violating the law.

A community would be wise to send new board members, at community expense, to the one-day course presented by the Chesapeake Region Chapter of the Community Associations Institute (CAI) introducing board members to association laws and association best practices. Not only will the new board member get useful information, he or she will have the opportunity to network with other new board members. Just listening to the questions fellow new board members raise in these sessions is an education in itself. A reference manual comes with the course. Go to the website of the Chesapeake Region Chapter of the Community Associations Institute (CAI) for a schedule of classes (www.caimsches.org). If going to a class is not a possibility, the national CAI organization has inexpensive training materials available online. Go to www.caionline.org and select Information & Tools.

I've attempted to cover sections of the Maryland Condominium Act and Maryland Homeowners Association Act that refer to everyday association governance. However, the laws are obviously much more robust, and there are sections that regulate situations that occur more rarely. I highly recommend that you turn to the text of the laws and perhaps even consult an attorney in these cases.

In summary, every homeowner is entitled to the peaceful enjoyment of his or her home. It is up to every individual living in a community to work toward making peaceful enjoyment a reality. I hope that *Happy Homes* makes this goal a little easier for each of you.

Appendix 1: Best Practices for Hiring a Management Company

It is estimated that 50 percent of Maryland condo and HOA associations are self-managed. In some self-managed associations, the board tries to do it all; in others, the board hires an accountant to handle the finances but the board itself solicits contractors and conducts the "policing" of the association.

Association self-management is a bad idea for several reasons. First, to do it properly a board must educate itself on all the facets of association management. Since self-management is hard work, board members burn out quickly, many times with no one willing to run for the board and replace them. In reality, a board is elected to be the decision-making and advisory group for the association, not the association's servants.

The money saved by not having the services of a manager is quickly lost by ill-informed board decisions. It takes a trained professional to deal with soliciting contractor bids, applying for Federal Housing Administration (FHA) financing certification, preparing the association's yearly income tax returns, and preparing past-due assessment notices. Further, it is the association manager who contacts residents when there are problems, rather than a board member. Thus, board members are insulated from the wrath of an angry resident who feels unfairly targeted. Good association managers are trained to be diplomatic and defuse volatile situations.

That said, boards must use great care selecting a management company. These companies handle millions of dollars of association money a year, and as of this writing Maryland does not license or regulate managers. However, legislation has been introduced every year for the past few years (including the 2014 legislative session) that would require licensure of association managers. Such licensing would ensure that association managers are appropriately trained and do not have criminal backgrounds. Licensing also means a manager's license can be revoked as a result of complaints against the manager. Maryland licenses manicurists. It seems ridiculous not to also license individuals who handle the finances for one of our biggest investments—our homes.

Hiring a trustworthy management company and careful monitoring of association financial records is a high priority for boards. Here are suggestions for what to look for when hiring a management company.

Services:

1. Get contract bids from three or more management companies and compare them carefully. Management fees vary greatly from company to company. A management agreement usually consists of the duties a manager will perform for the monthly compensation agreed upon. There is also a section called "Nonroutine Services and Fees" listing all the services that will be billed separately as special projects. The cost of such nonroutine services can really add up. When you are comparing the monthly cost of management companies, make sure you estimate what the nonroutine services will cost you and add that to the yearly compensation. Only

then can you compare the costs of a company that provides all services for a monthly fee with a company that has many services they call nonroutine. You may find that a company with a higher monthly fee is actually cheaper in the long run.

2. Ask for examples of all routine ("form") letters that the company uses to communicate with the community and vendors as well as samples of its management reports. Hold on to these so that you can use them as examples of the services you were promised.

3. Only hire a management company that will give the board electronic read-only access to all association accounts or is willing to have the bank mail copies of the association's bank statements and canceled check images directly to the board treasurer. Unfortunately, some management companies have electronically altered account information in order to embezzle funds. A Maryland management company that was recently forced to close was expert in altering association bank statements. Most banks charge only $5.00 a month for up to ten people to have electronic read-only access to the association account records. Thus, there is no reason why the entire board can't monitor association funds rather than just the treasurer.

4. Review the management contract carefully. The manager is obliged to perform only those tasks listed in the contract. The association will be charged for any additional services. Make sure the community understands that the manager is required to do only what is specified in the contract. Unfortunately, some homeowners feel that the manager should do whatever they request, and that is just not so. An example of an unreasonable demand occurs when a homeowner with expertise in

accounting asks for nonstandard financial reports for his or her personal use. An individual who wants this information can create it from the association's monthly financial reports or, alternatively, mobilize the community to ask the board to pay the management company for this extra report.

5. Make sure the management contract does not have a section restricting your ability to cancel the contract. Thirty days written notice with or without cause is appropriate and common.

Credentials:

6. Most management companies give their managers extensive Community Associations Institute (CAI) training. These CAI accredited managers have the letters AMS, PCAM, or AAMC behind their names. Check the CAI website to make sure your prospective manager actually has the credentials indicated. If you hire a manager without training, you are taking a big risk with the security of your association.

7. Check the management company's references and contact homeowners who live in other associations it manages to get their opinion.

8. Do a Better Business Bureau and/or Maryland Judiciary Case Search of the company. (See the Resources section at the end of this book for contact information.) Are there complaints or major lawsuits pending against this firm?

9. The board should interview the actual manager who will be assigned to your association, not just the spokesperson for the company. Make sure the potential manager understands that he or she is advisory to the board

and should speak at board meetings only when asked to do so. You want a manager who is knowledgeable yet does not undercut the authority of the board.

10. Find out the procedure for replacing the assigned manager if there's a problem.

Monitoring:

11. Poll the community regularly about the service they are receiving from the manager.

12. If you find your newly hired manager is not satisfactory, contact the president of the management company and ask for a new manager before you look for another company.

Appendix 2: Best Practices for Hiring an Attorney

Hiring a well-trained and ethical attorney to advise the association is, next to hiring a good management company, one of the most important decisions a board will make. If your candidate can't explain Maryland law and your governing documents to you in language you can understand, don't hire him or her. The following attorney interview questions are designed to help you determine whether a particular attorney has the association's best interests at heart or will just run up attorney fees.

1. What is your training in homeowner association law and do you represent both associations and individual owners? What is your track record with respect to defending owners as well as appealing adverse decisions?
2. Can you provide references from associations?
3. Do you provide the board with easy-to-understand updates to Maryland law? How often? Can you provide us with examples?
4. What are your rates and how will you bill us?
5. Are you familiar with alternative dispute resolution procedures and mediation for resolving disputes? (An attorney who only knows how to take owners to court will cost much more than someone who is trained in mediating disputes.)

6. Do you resolve some cases in small claims court?
7. Is your firm licensed as a collection agency in Maryland? If so, what procedures do you follow when collecting past-due fees?
8. Will junior attorneys or paralegals handle some of the administrative work at a lower cost?
9. Do you require a retainer?
10. Can you give me an estimate of the total bill and fees for a particular case?
11. How will you keep the association informed of the progress of a case and how frequently?
12. Do you carry professional liability insurance and may we have a copy of your certificate of insurance?
13. What will you expect of the board should we decide to retain you as legal counsel?

Before hiring anyone, check to see if the attorney you are considering has been sanctioned by the Maryland Attorney Grievance Commission. (See the Resources section at the end of this book for contact information.) If you have questions regarding the licensure of the attorney or questions of ethics and qualifications, look up the individual on the Maryland State Bar Association's website. See the Resources section at the end of this book for complete contact information.

Resources

Maryland Condominium Act
Maryland Homeowners Association Act
Go to the General Assembly of Maryland web site (http://
mgaleg.maryland.gov/webmga/frm1st.aspx?tab=home) and
select the Statutes tab and then the LexisNexis link in the
bottom left corner of the Statutes page. Agree to the terms
presented, then click the plus sign next to "Real Property" to
open a menu of more selections. To access the MCA, click
the plus sign next to "Title 11. Maryland Condominium
Act." To access the MHAA, click the plus sign next to "Title
11B. Maryland Homeowners Association Act."

Maryland Homeowners' Association, Inc.
4300 Montgomery Avenue, Suite 205
Bethesda, MD 20814
301-654-9242
    e-mail: mail@marylandhomeownersassociation.info
    website: www.marylandhomeownersassociation.info

Chesapeake Region Chapter of the Community Associations
Institute (CAI)
1985 Fairfax Road
Annapolis, MD 21401
410-540-9831
e-mail: contact@caimdches.org
website: www.caimdches.org (Chesapeake Region Chapter)

www.caionline.org (national site; to access the CAI Bookstore, click the Information & Tools tab on the home page)

For mediation services, contact the **Maryland Mediation and Conflict Resolution Office (MACRO)** of the Maryland Courts.
MACRO
903 Commerce Road
Annapolis, MD 21401
410-260-3540
    e-mail: macro@mdcourts.gov
    website: www.courts.state.md.us/macro

Consumer Financial Protection Bureau
This federal bureau is interested in debt collection problems such as collection of assessments. You can file a complaint or just tell your story online.
855-411-2372
website: www.consumerfinance.gov

Office of the Maryland Attorney General, Consumer Protection Division
If your association is violating the MCA or the MHAA, you can file a complaint with this office. Complaints may be filed online or by U.S. mail.

Consumer Protection Division
    Office of the Maryland Attorney General
    200 Saint Paul Place
    Baltimore, MD 21202
Consumer Hotline: 410-528-8662
website: www.oag.state.md.us/Consumer

If you live in **Prince George's County**, you can seek help from the **Office of Common Ownership Communities.**

Common Ownership Communities
301-952-4729 (this is also the number to call for neighbor-to-neighbor mediation)
e-mail: COC@co.pg.md.us
website: http://www.princegeorgescountymd.gov/Pages/default.aspx (if a user name/password screen comes up, select Cancel and the web page will appear; select My Community, then Services, then Community Affairs Division.
   Common Ownership Communities
   Email: COC@co.pg.md.us
301-952-4729
For Neighbor-to-Neighbor Mediation, call this same number, 301-952-4729

If you live in **Montgomery County** and you are concerned about actions by your board, or you are a board concerned about the action of a homeowner, you can contact the **Commission on Common Ownership Communities**.

Commission on Common Ownership Communities
240-777-3636
website: www.montgomerycountymd.gov/ocp/ (select Common Ownership Communities)

If you live in **Charles County**, you can file a complaint with the **Charles County Homeowner's Association Dispute Review Board.**

Charles County Homeowner's Association Dispute Review Board
    PO Box 2150 (mailing address)
    200 Baltimore Street (street address)
    La Plata, MD 20646
    301-645-0550 or 301-870-3000

If you live in **Howard County**, you can file a complaint with the **Howard County Office of Consumer Affairs** if your complaint involves unfair or deceptive trade practices by your developer or if you have questions about or need help with a home improvement contractor or other service provider.
Howard County Office of Consumer Affairs
6751 Columbia Gateway Drive
Columbia, MD 21046
410-313-6420
    e-mail: consumer@howardcountymd.gov
    website: www.howardcountymd.gov/consumer

If you have been threatened with foreclosure because of unpaid assessments, the **Maryland Foreclosure Prevention Service** staff may be able to provide help through its **Home Owners Preserving Equity Initiative**.

Maryland Foreclosure Prevention Service
    100 Community Place
    Crownsville, MD 21032
    MD HOPE Hotline: 877-462-7555
    e-mail: customerservice@mdhousing.org
    website: www.mdhope.dhcd.maryland.gov

If you feel you are being discriminated against by your association or by your association manager, you can file a complaint with the **Maryland Commission on Civil Rights**.

Maryland Commission on Civil Rights
6 Saint Paul Street, Suite 900
Baltimore, MD 21202-1631
800-637-6247 or 410-767-8600
website: www.mccr.maryland.gov

If you feel you are getting misleading property insurance information from your board, property manager, or insurance agent, you can contact the **Maryland Insurance Administration**.

Maryland Insurance Administration
200 Saint Paul Place, Suite 2700
Baltimore, MD 21202
800-492-6116 or 410-468-2000
website: www.mdinsurance.state.md.us/sa/jsp/Mia.jsp

If you or your community feels you are getting unprofessional legal services, you may file a complaint against your attorney with the **Attorney Grievance Commission** or check the **Maryland State Bar Association**.
Attorney Grievance Commission
People's Resource Center, Suite 3301
100 Community Place
Crownsville, MD 21032
410-514-7051
e-mail: AGCMD@mdcourts.gov
website: www.courts.state.md.us/attygrievance

Maryland State Bar Association, Inc.
520 W. Fayette Street
Baltimore, MD 21201
800-492-1964 or 410-685-7878, 800-492-1964
e-mail: webmaster@msba.org
website: www.msba.org

If you are looking for a consumer-friendly attorney to represent you, you might contact a Maryland attorney listed in the directory of the **National Association of Consumer Advocates**.
National Association of Consumer Advocates
1730 Rhode Island Avenue NW, Suite 710
Washington, DC 20036
202-452-1989
e-mail: info@naca.net
website: www.naca.net

If you have a complaint about a CAI-certified association manager, you can contact **CAI's Community Association Managers International Certification Board**.
CEO, CAI
6402 Arlington Boulevard, Suite 510
Falls Church, VA 22042
866-779-2622
e-mail: info@camicb.org
website: www.camicb.org/program/standards.cfm
(complaint form at the bottom of the page)

To see if any complaints have been registered against any service provider you are considering hiring, contact the consumer protection agencies listed here and contact the **Better Business Bureau**.

Better Business Bureau
502 S. Sharp Street, Suite 1200
Baltimore, MD 21201
410-347-3990
website: www.greatermd.bbb.org

To check on the credentials of potential contractors, go
to the **Maryland Department of Labor, Licensing and
Regulation**. Associations should avoid hiring unlicensed,
uninsured contractors.
Maryland Department of Labor, Licensing and Regulation
500 North Calvert Street, #401
Baltimore, MD 21202
410-230-6001
website: www.dllr.state.md.us/ (select Occupational and
Professional Licensing)

To determine if there are any lawsuits pending against a
service provider you are considering, you can do an online
search of the **Maryland Judiciary's Case Search** records
online. For directions for how to do a search, go to www.
mdcourts.gov and select Search Court Records.

To see if a lien has been placed on your property, go to
MDLANDREC, a digital image retrieval system for land
records in Maryland. You must register and agree to certain
conditions to use this system.
website: www.mdlandrec.net

To check on the credentials of people you are considering
for tree maintenance, there are two organizations you can go
to:
Maryland Department of Natural Resources

580 Taylor Avenue
Annapolis, MD 21401
877-620-8367
 e-mail: customerservice@dnr.state.md.us
 website: www.dnr.state.md.us

Maryland Arborist Association
 PO Box 712
 Brooklandville, MD 21022
410-321-8082
 e-mail: mdarboristassoc@aol.com
 website: www.mdarborist.com

Jeanne Ketley &
Belle

About the Author

After retiring from the NIH, Jeanne N. Ketley, PhD, joined the Maryland Homeowners' Association (MHA) in August 2004; she has been president of the MHA for the past five years. MHA is a consumer advocacy group dedicated to promoting the rights of unit owners and homeowners who belong to condominium and homeowner associations. She has been chairperson of the MHA Legislative Action Committee and editor of the MHA *E-Communicator*.

Dr. Ketley has a PhD from The Johns Hopkins School of Medicine. After a career in biomedical research, she became a scientific review administrator in the NIH Center for Scientific Review (CSR); she later retired from CSR as chief of the Cardiovascular Sciences Initial Review Group.

Dr. Ketley serves on her condominium's board of directors. She is married and has one son.